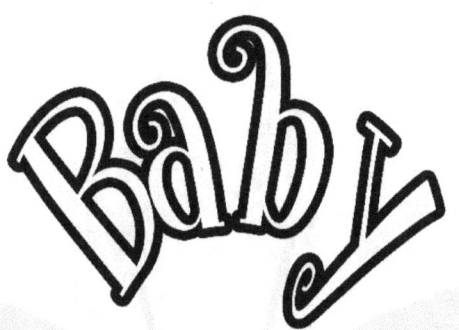

Baby
Valentine's Day Coloring Book

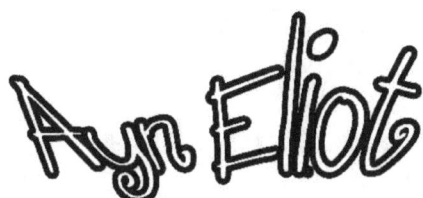

Ayn Eliot

Happy Coloring

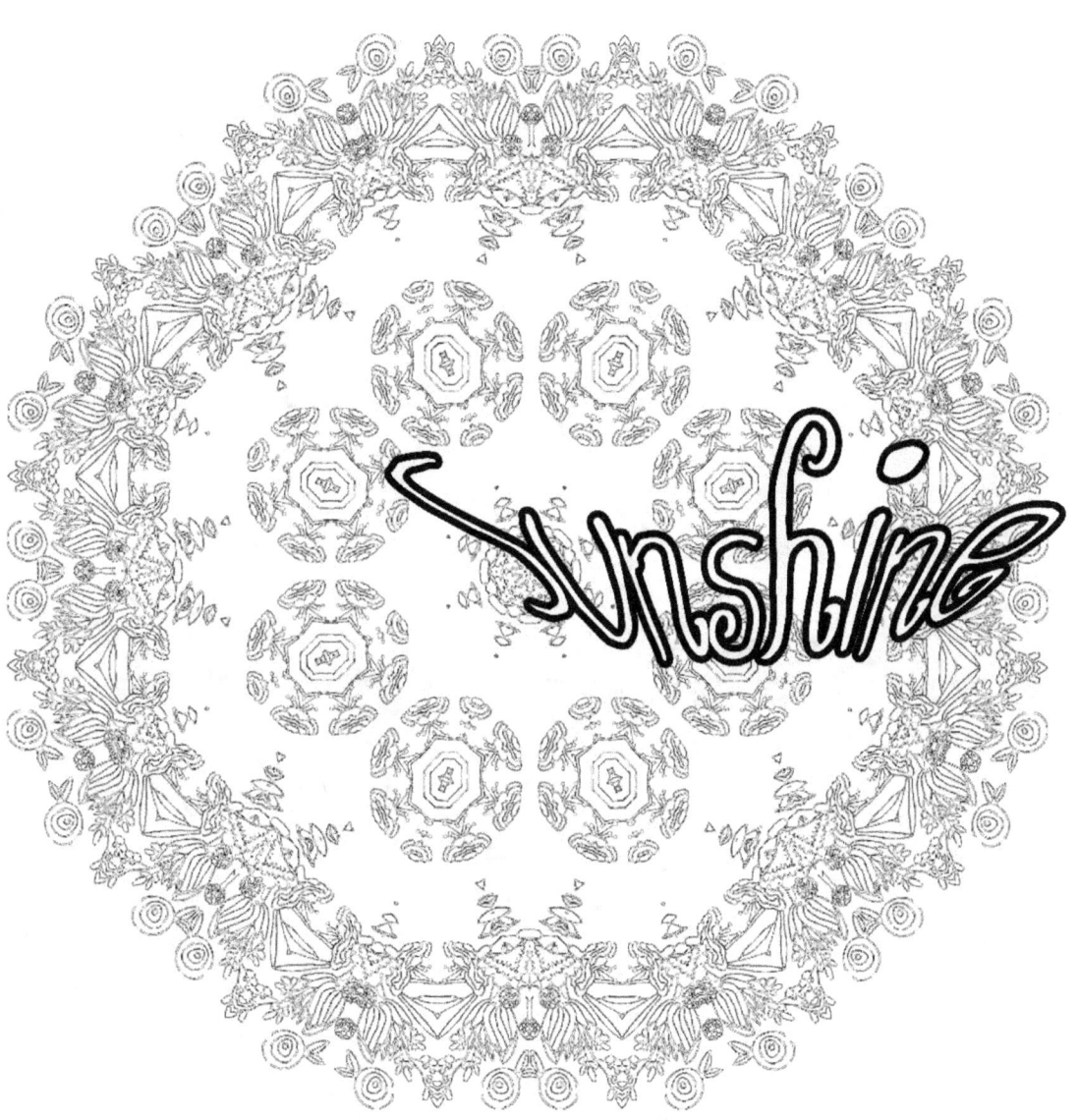

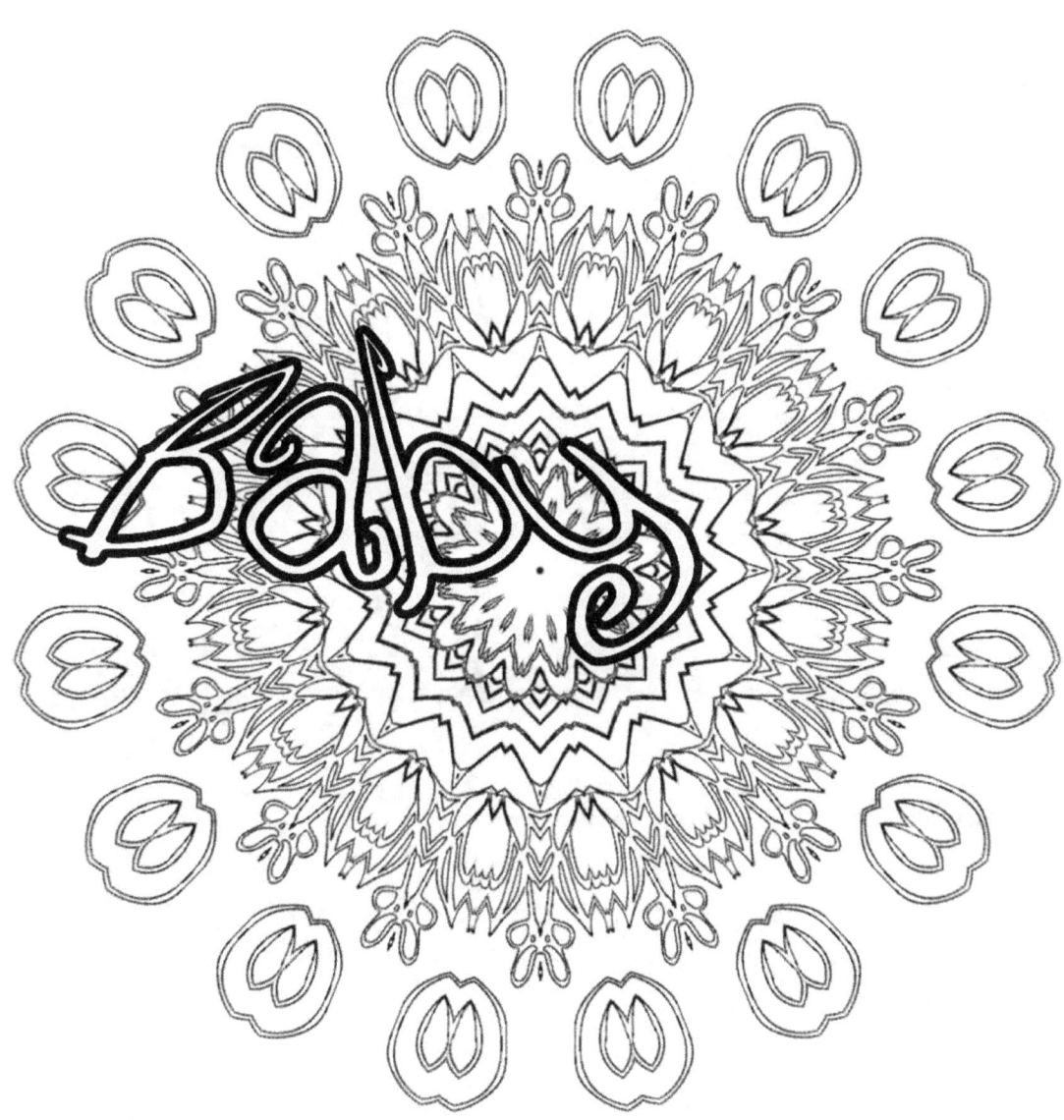

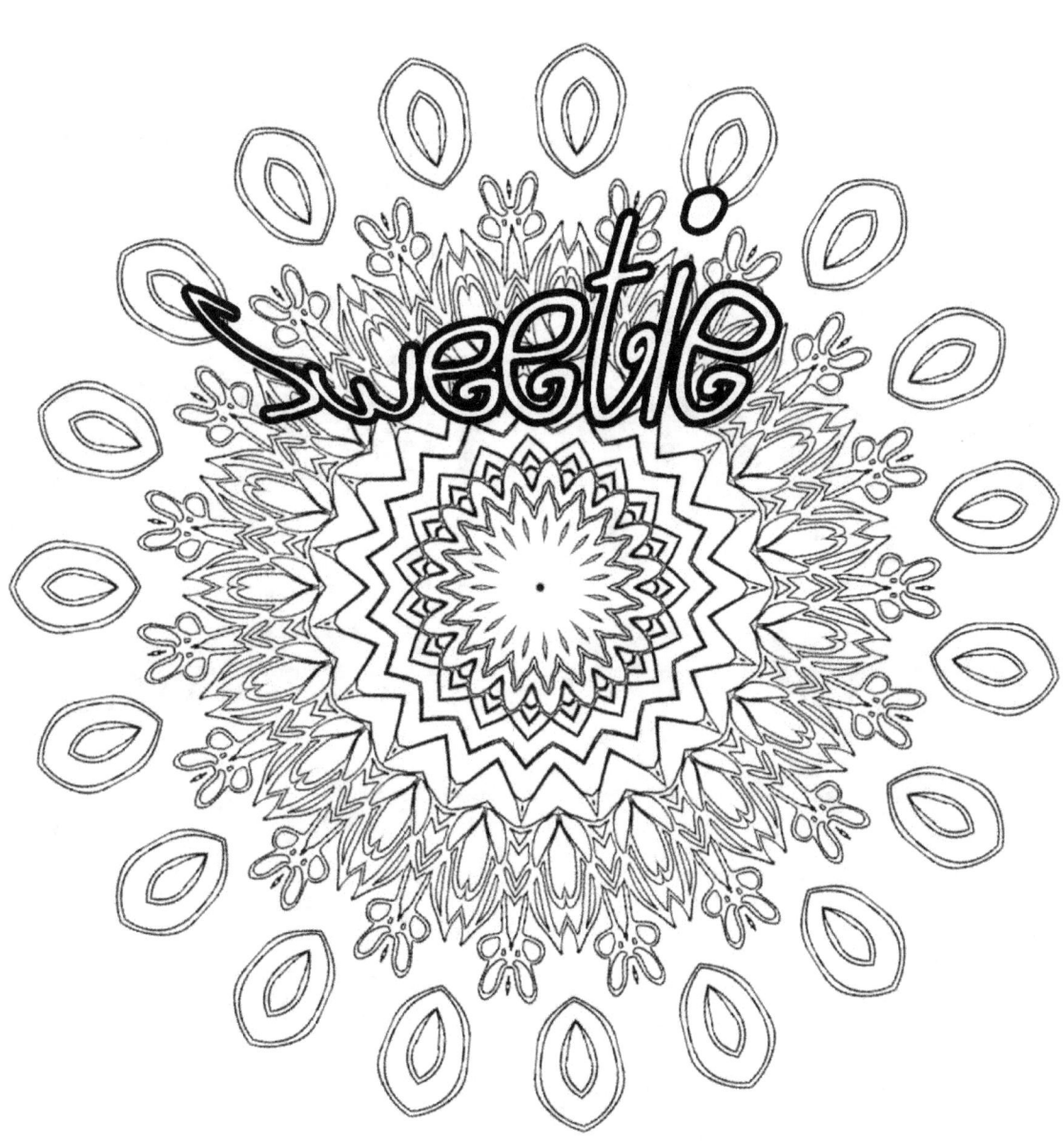

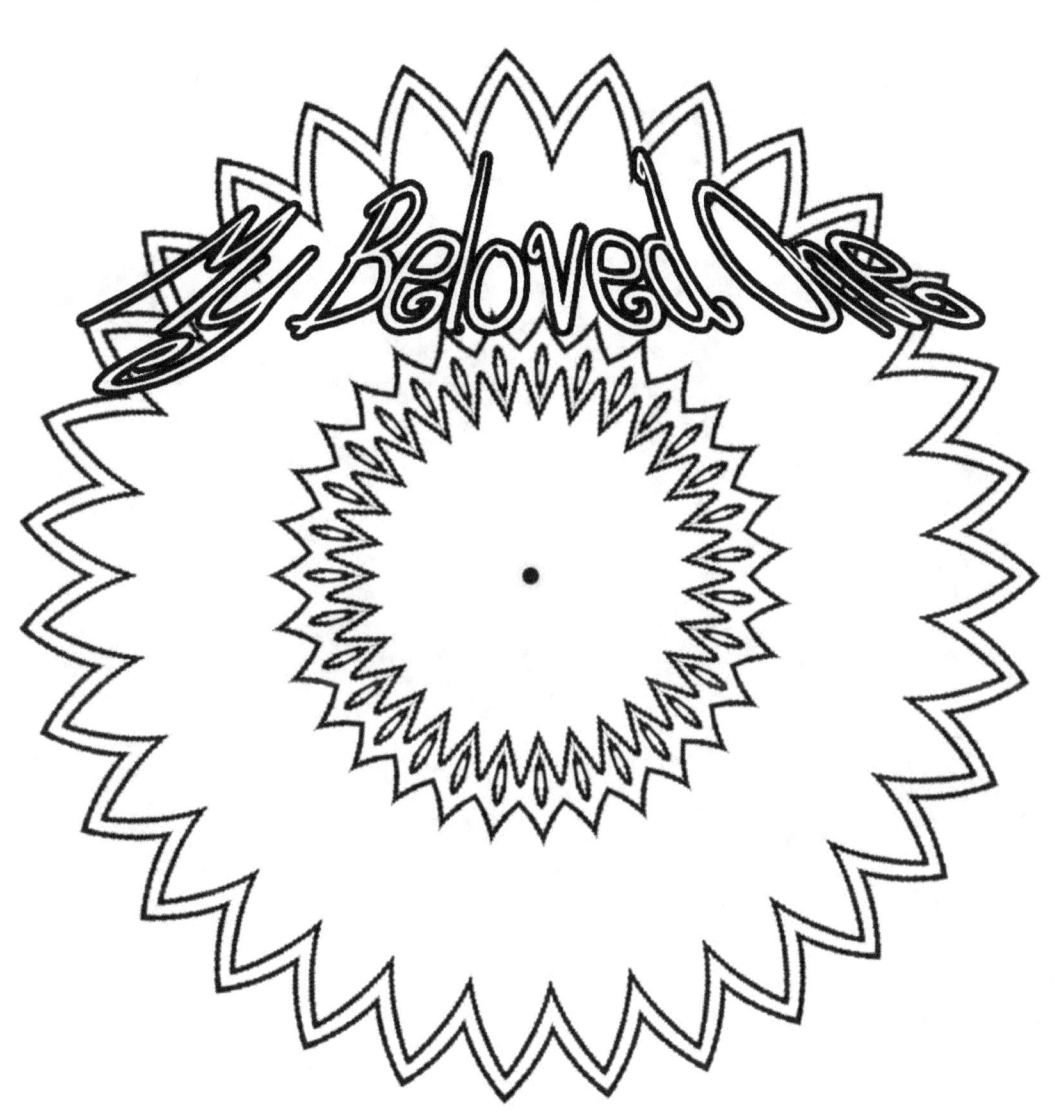

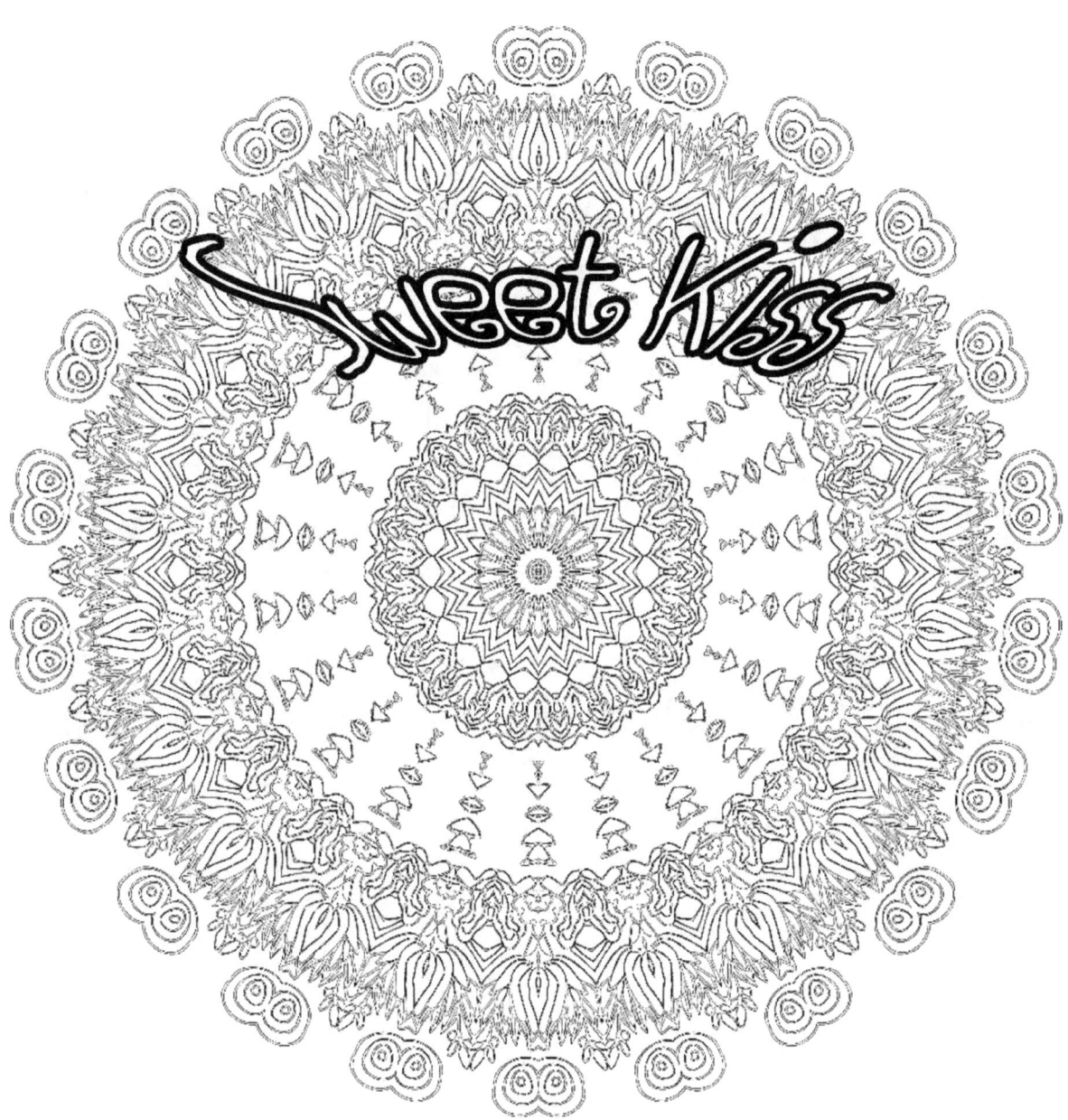

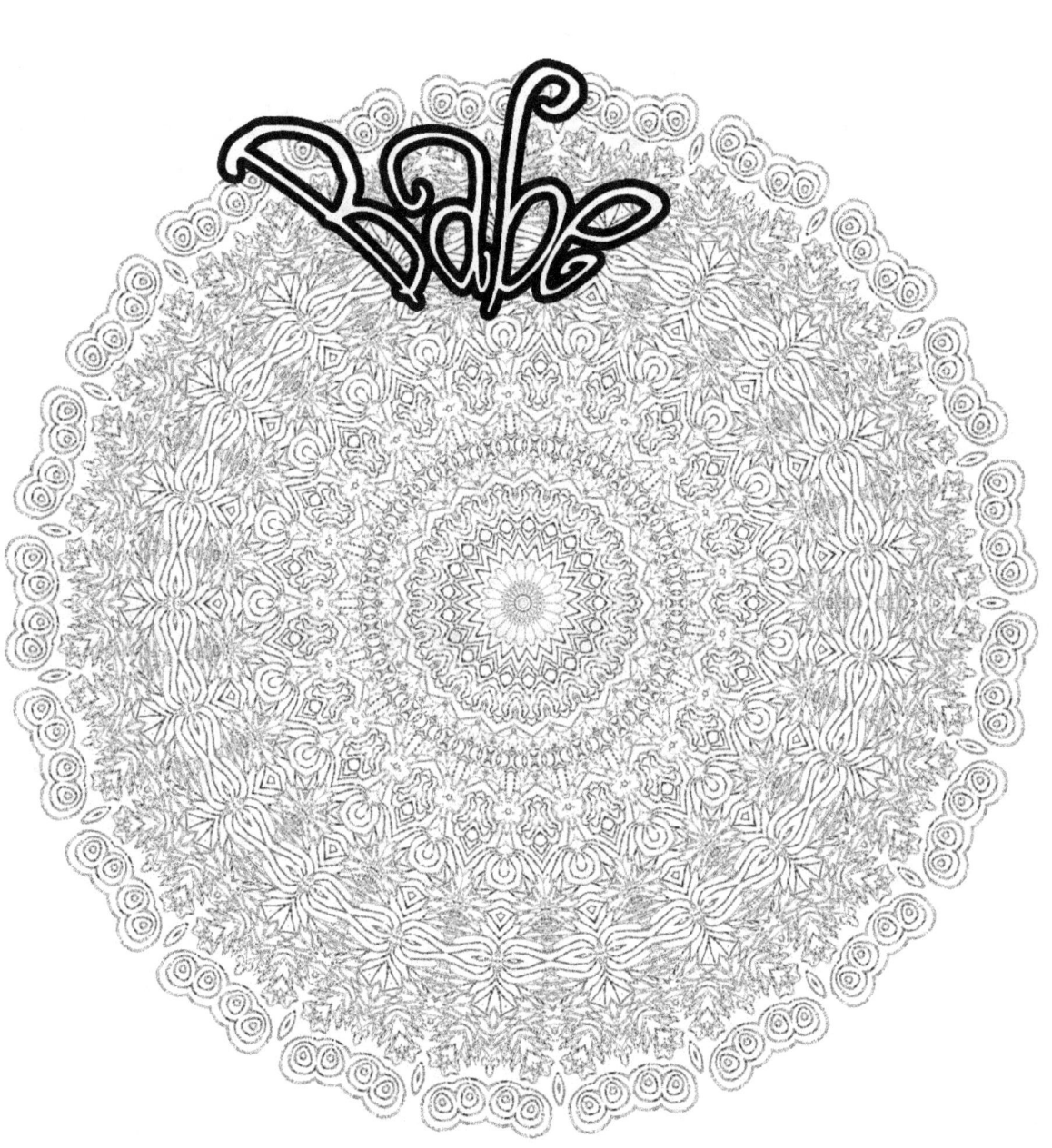

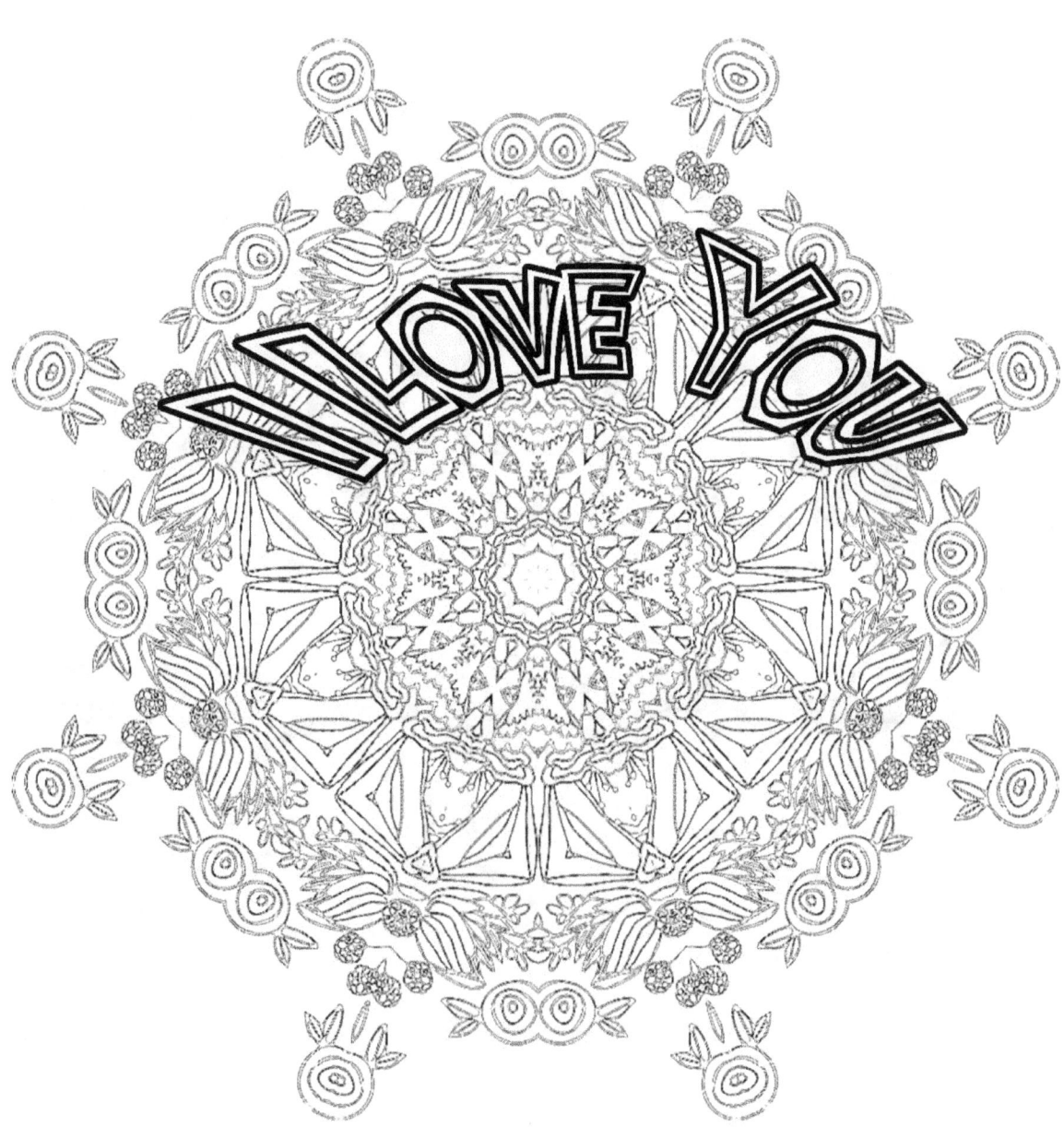

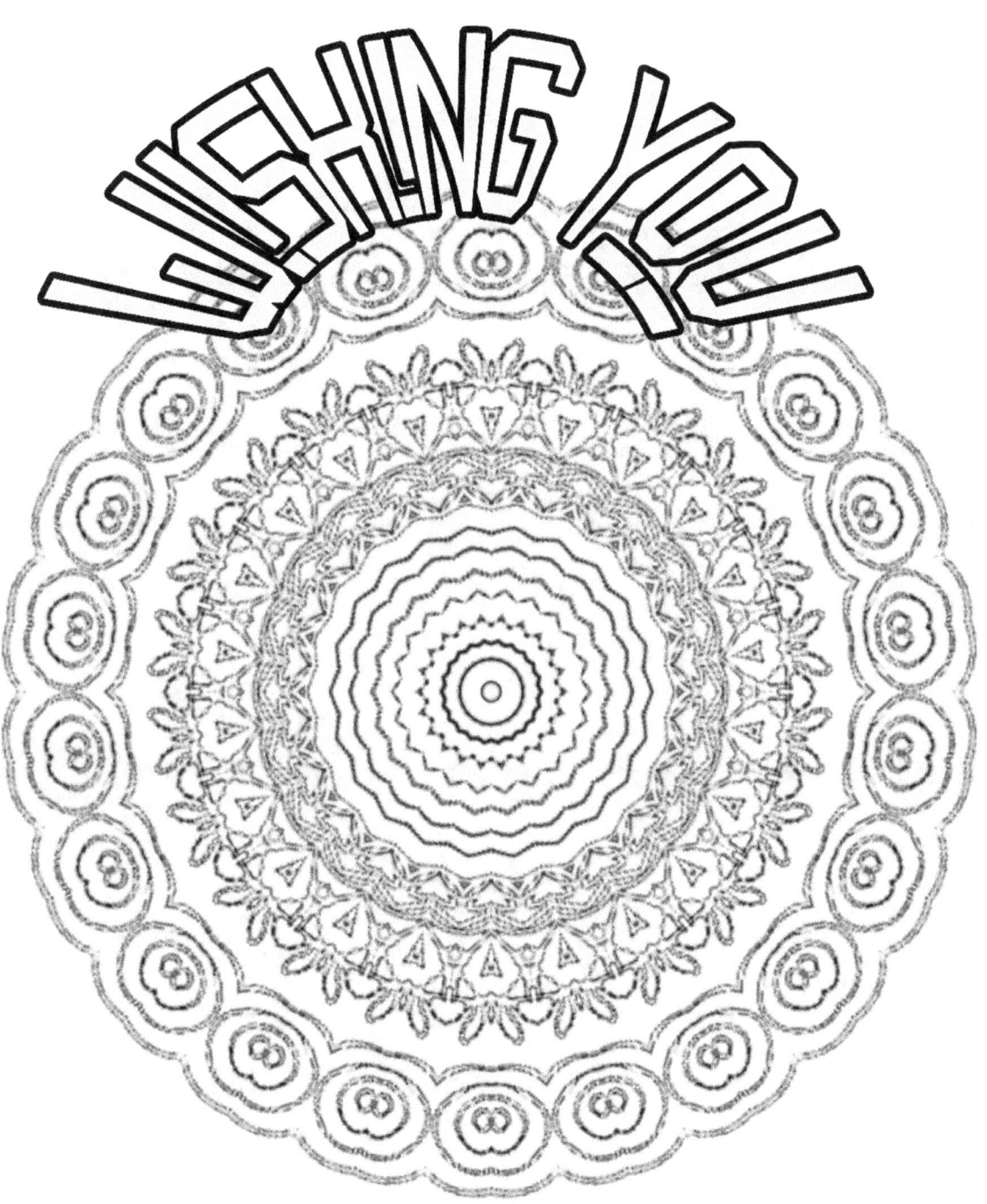

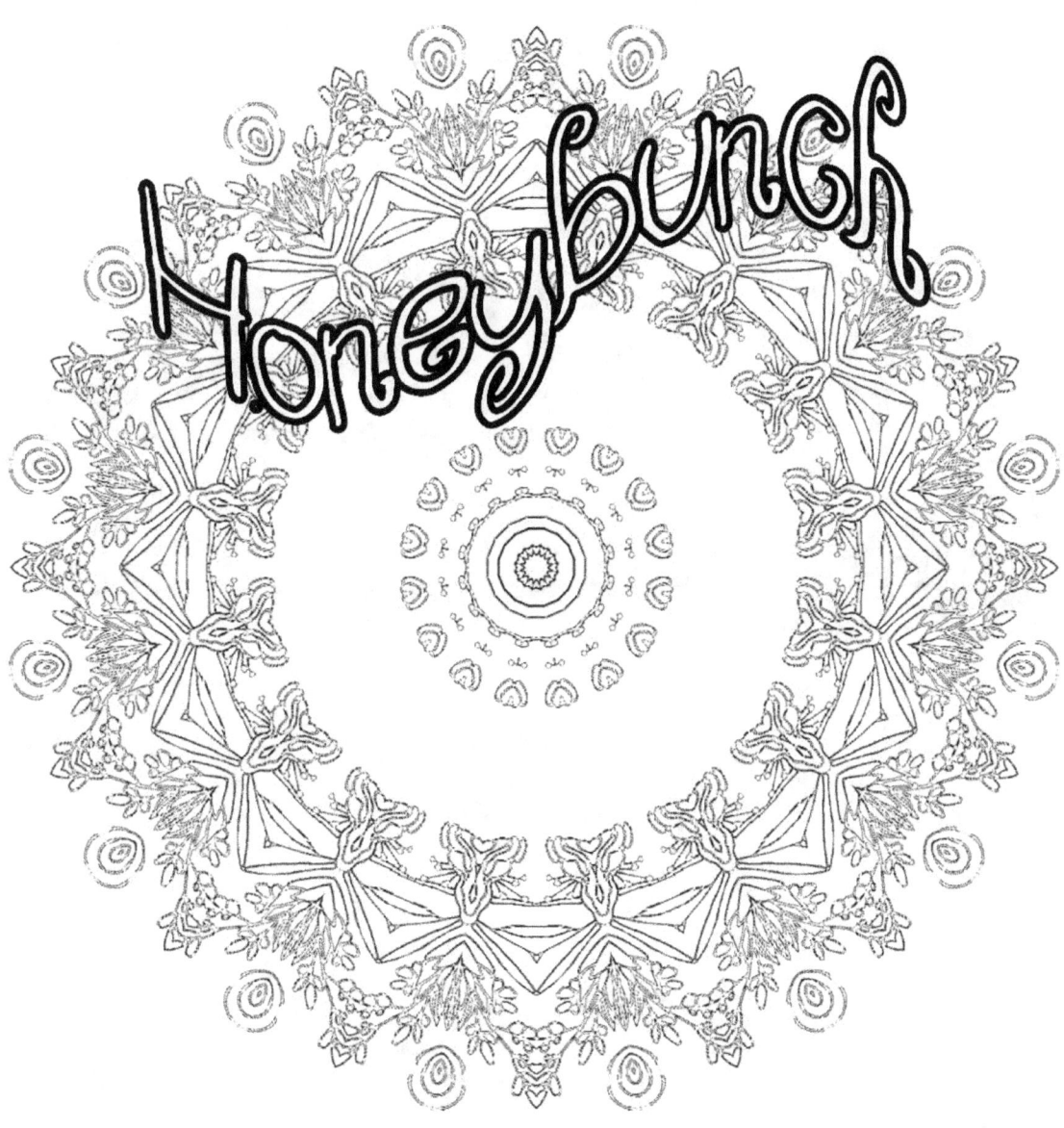

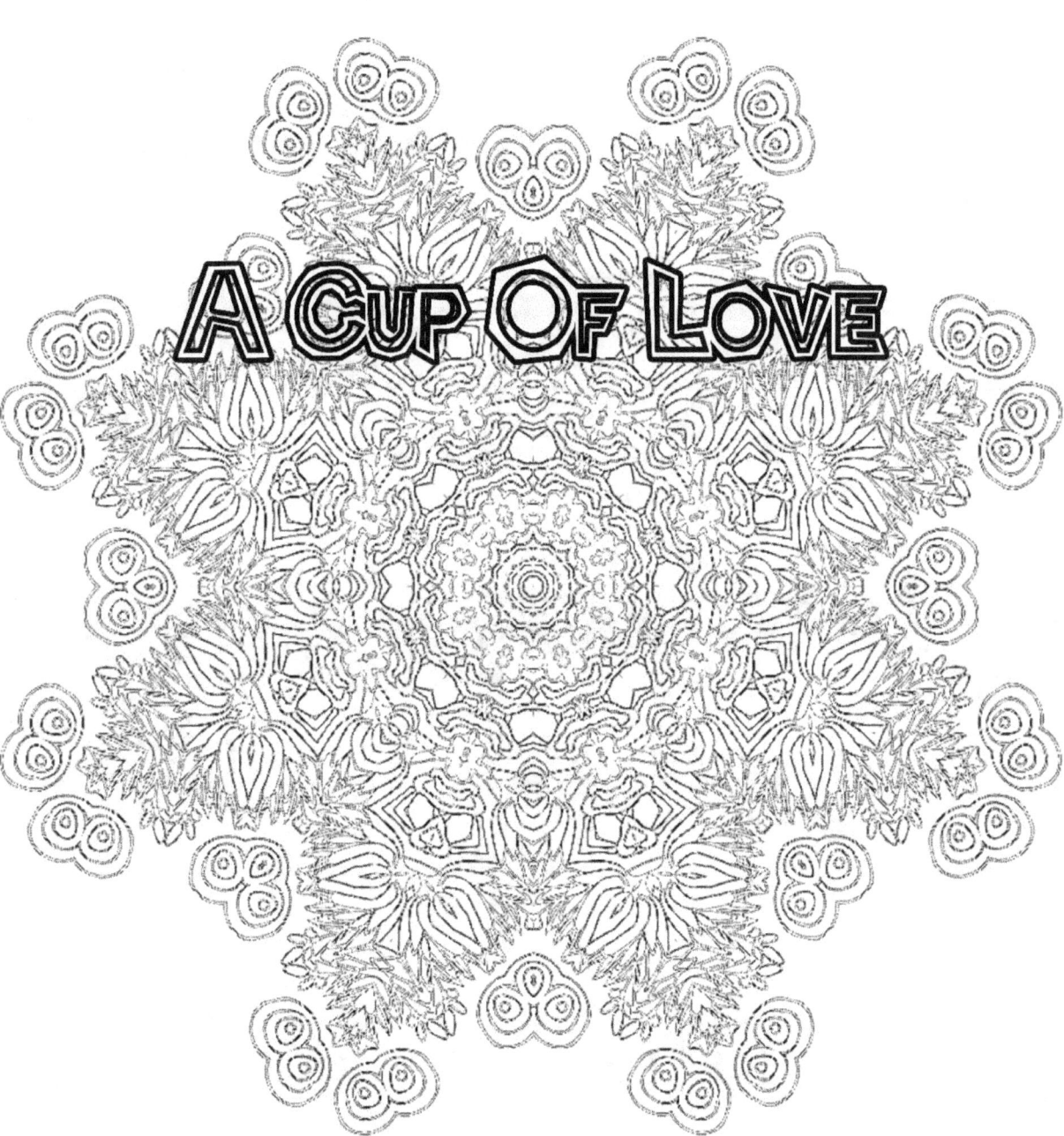

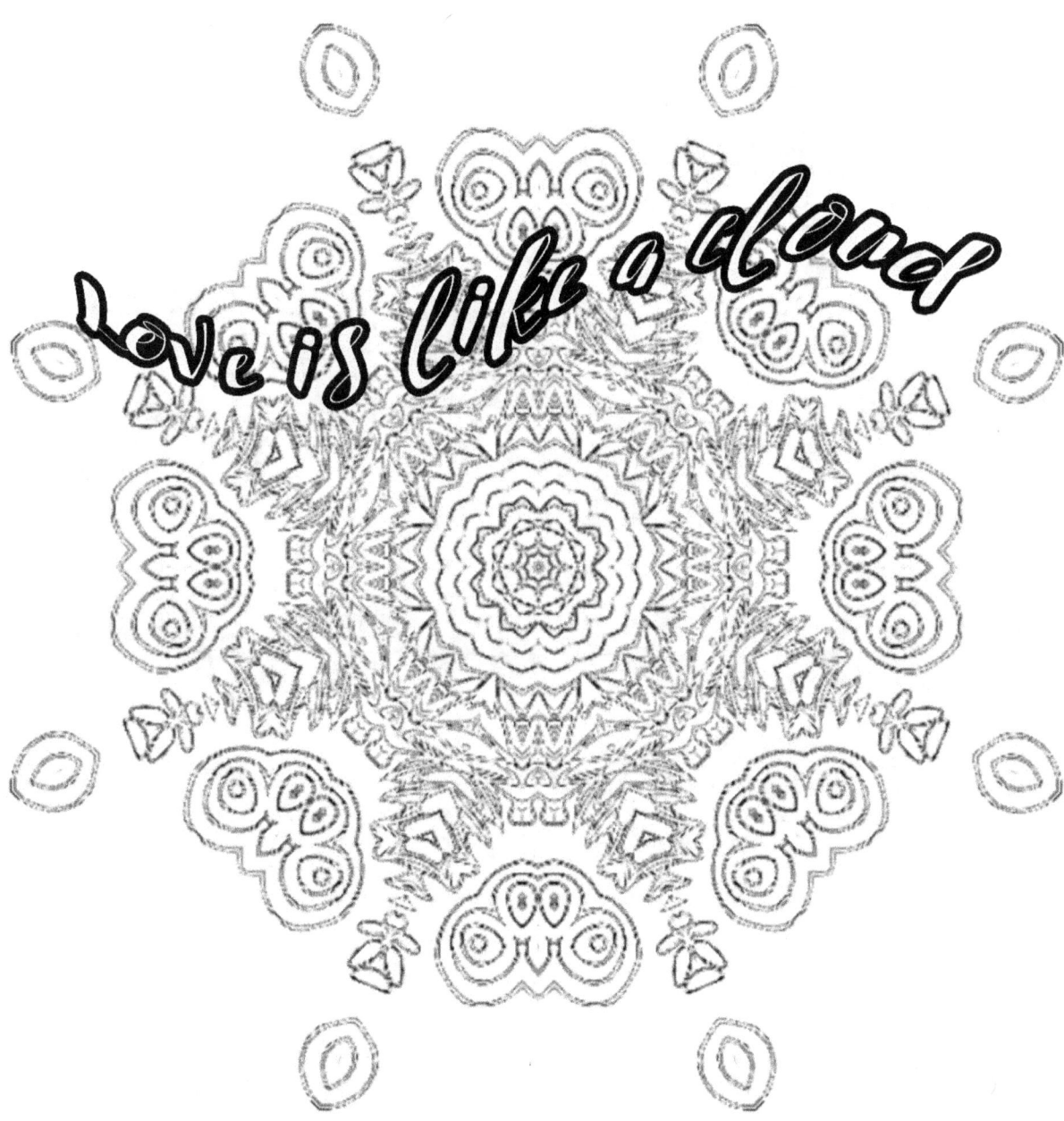

love is like a cloud

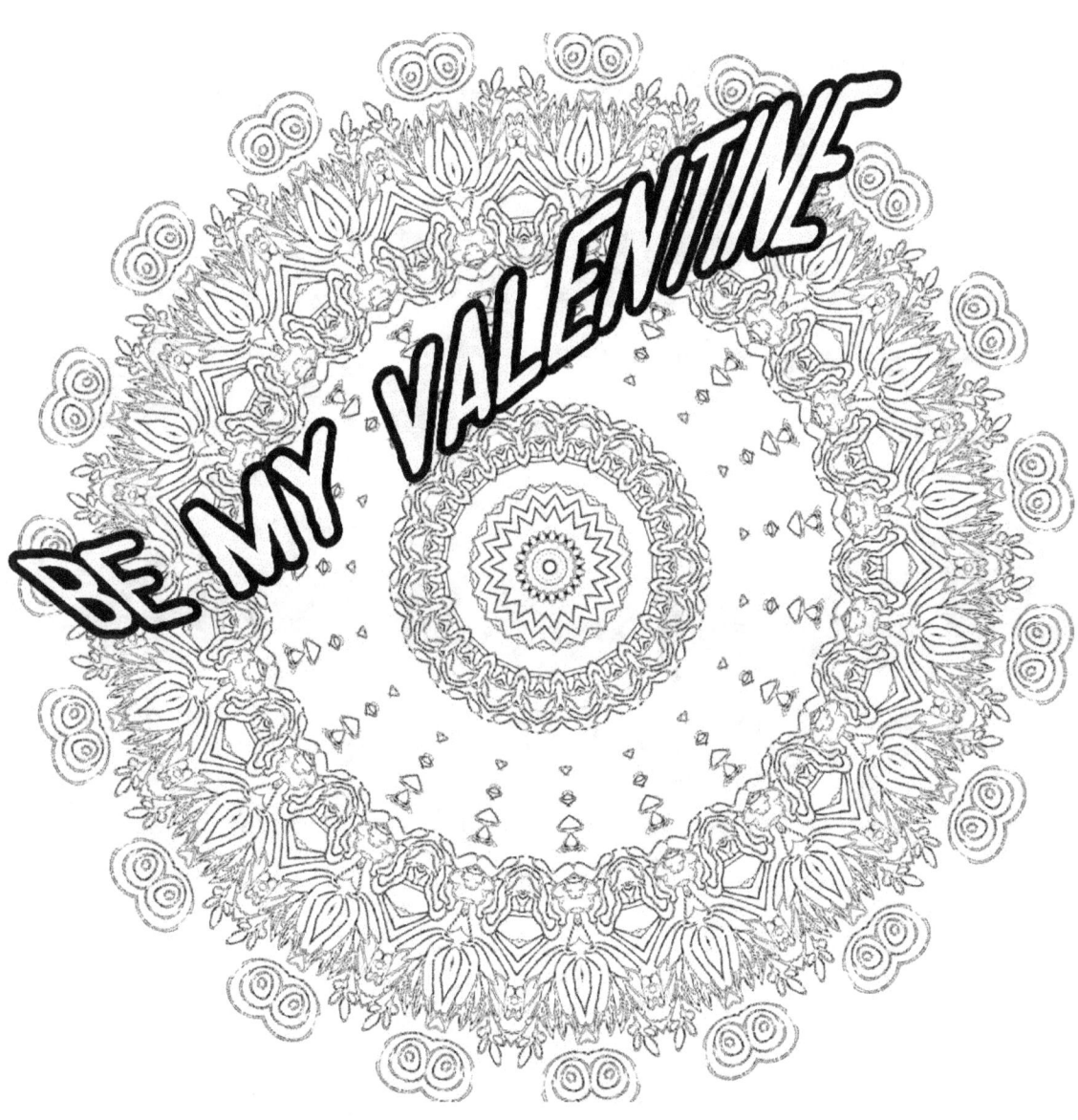

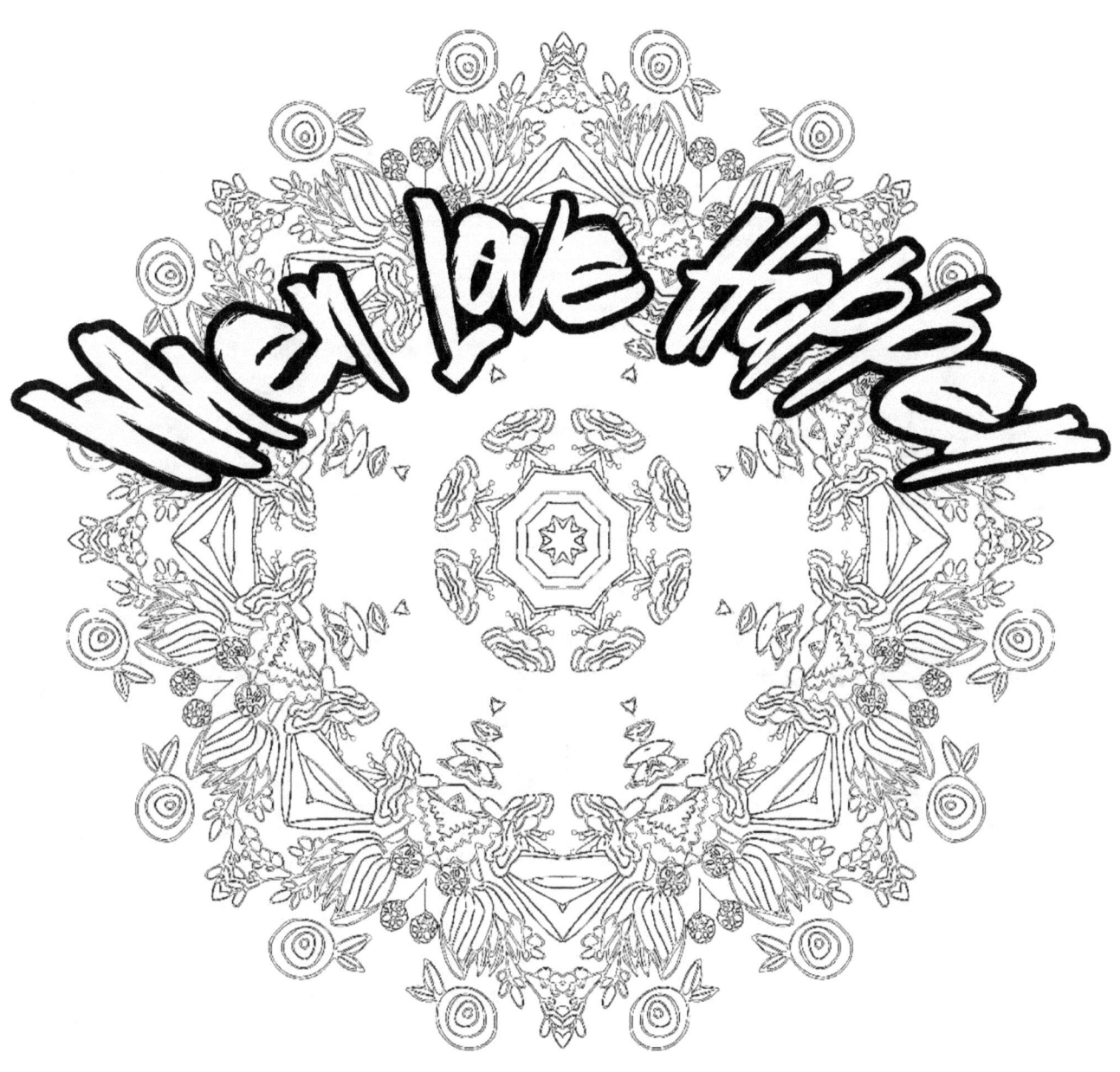

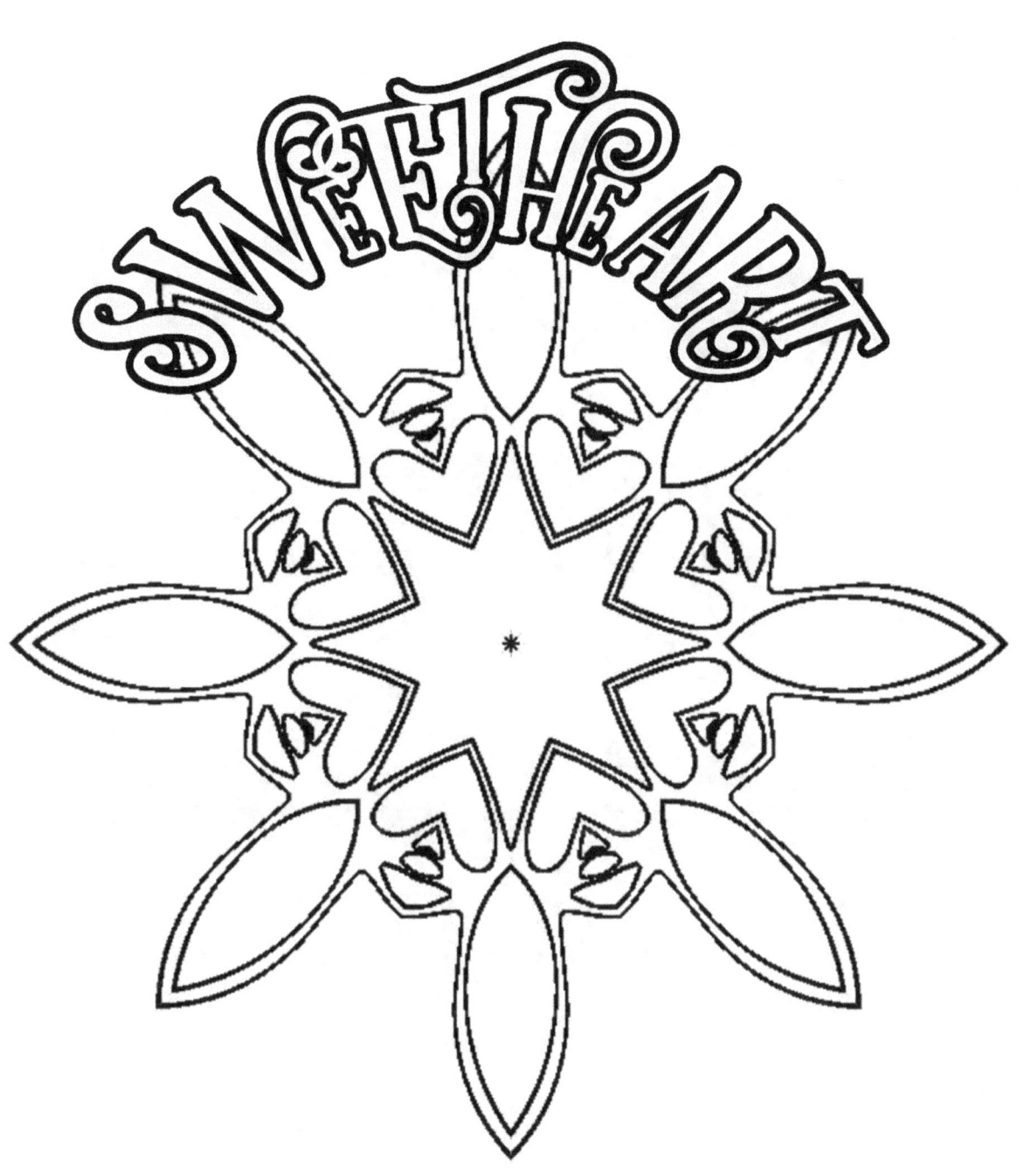

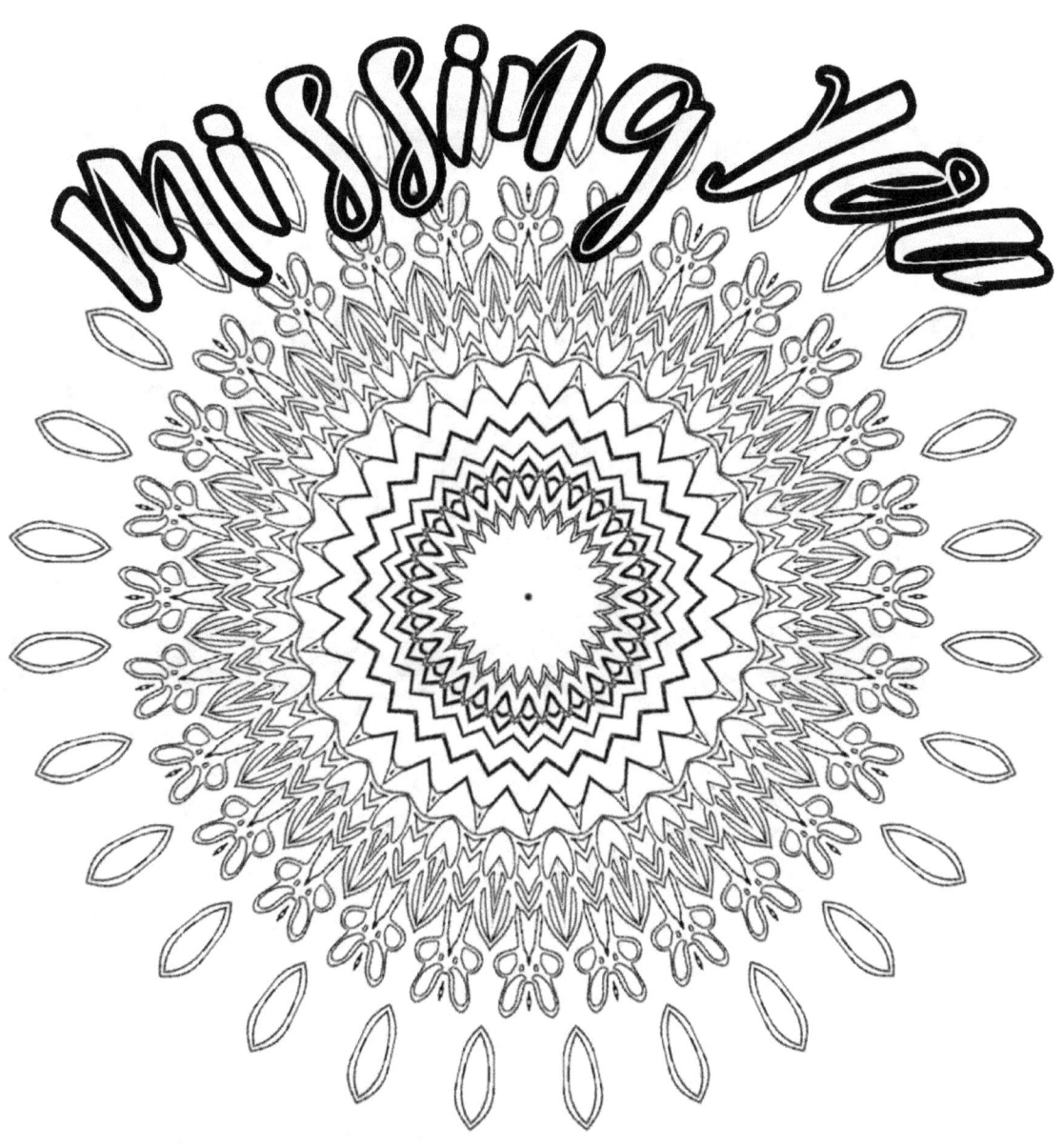

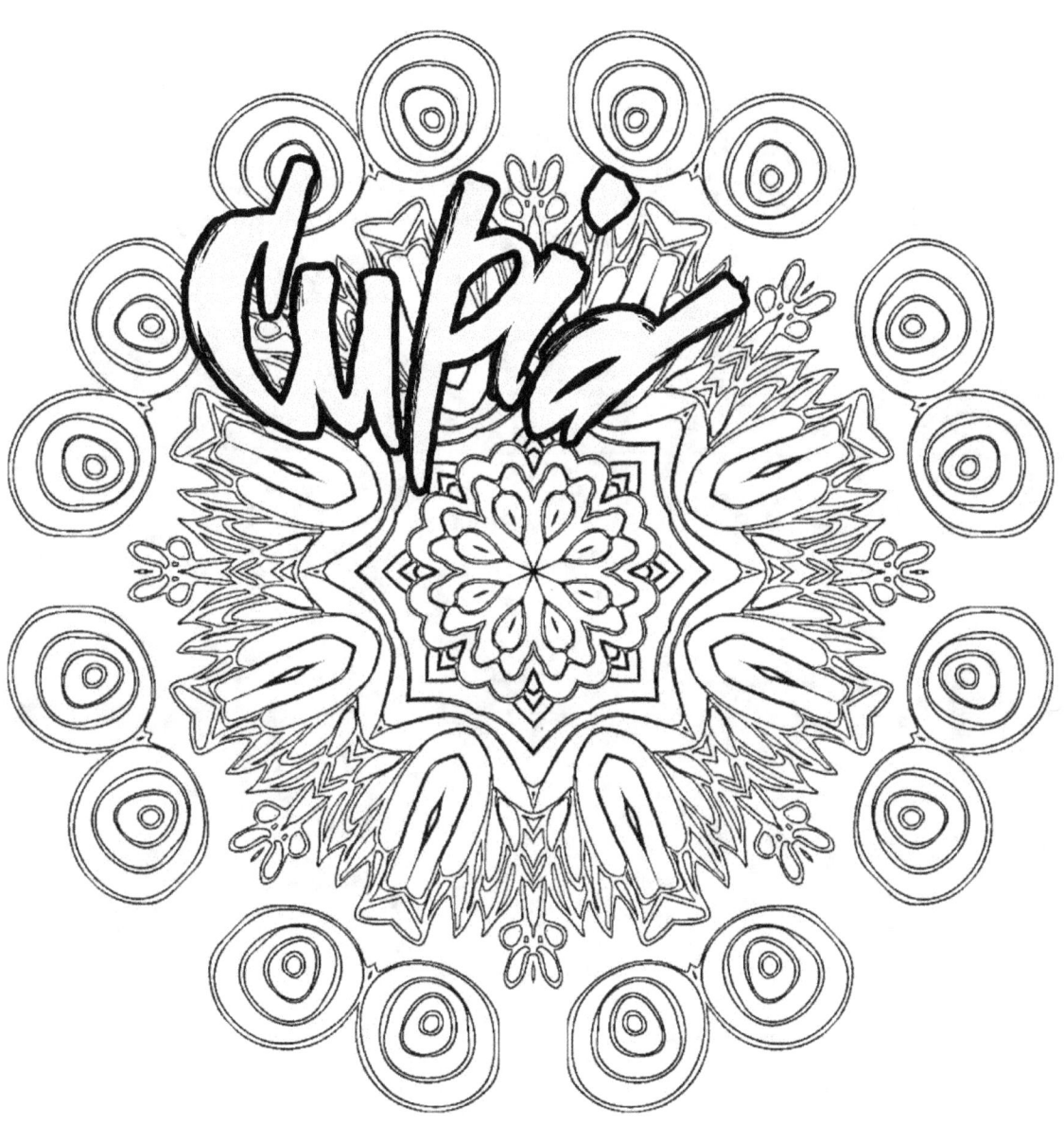

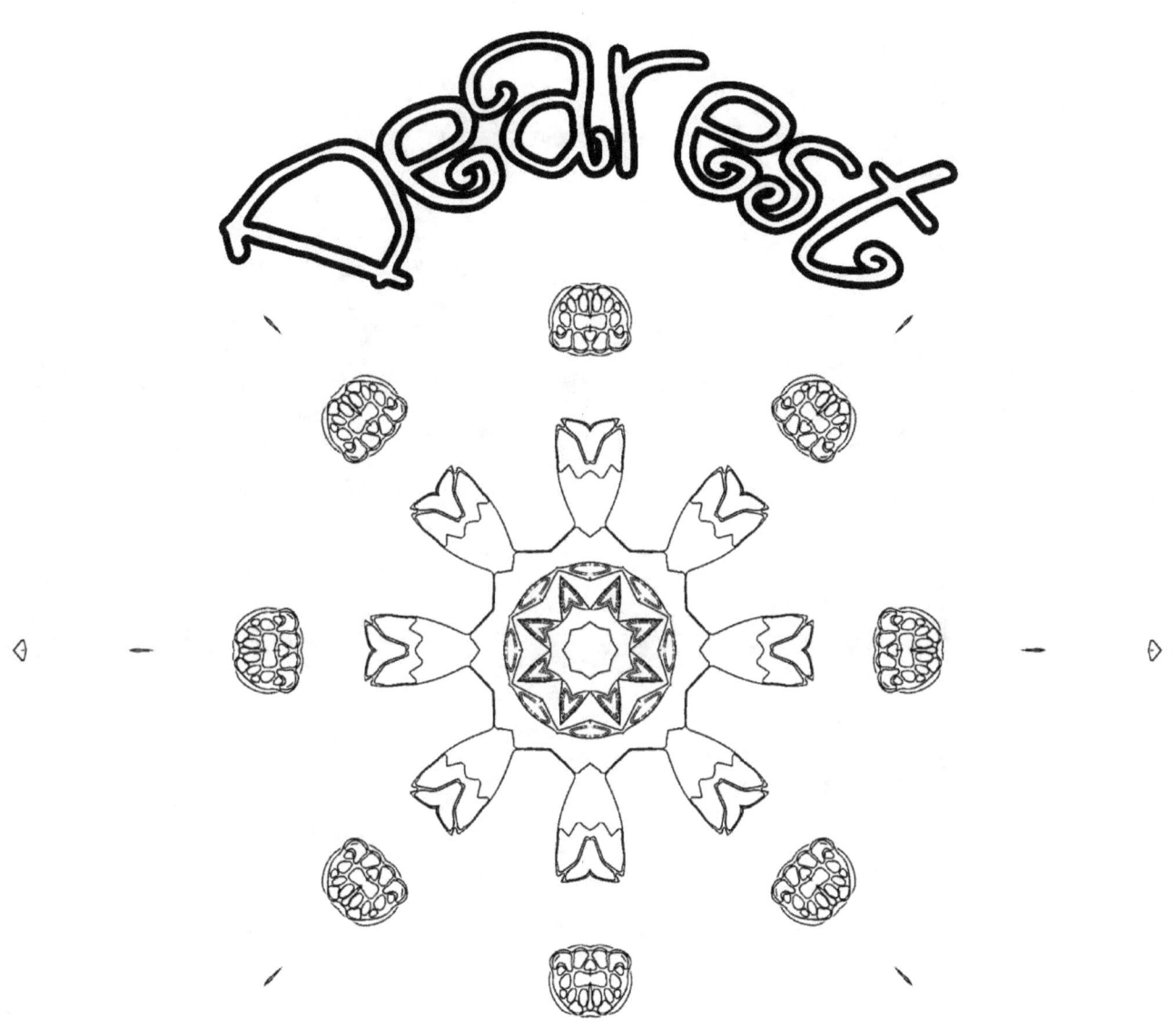

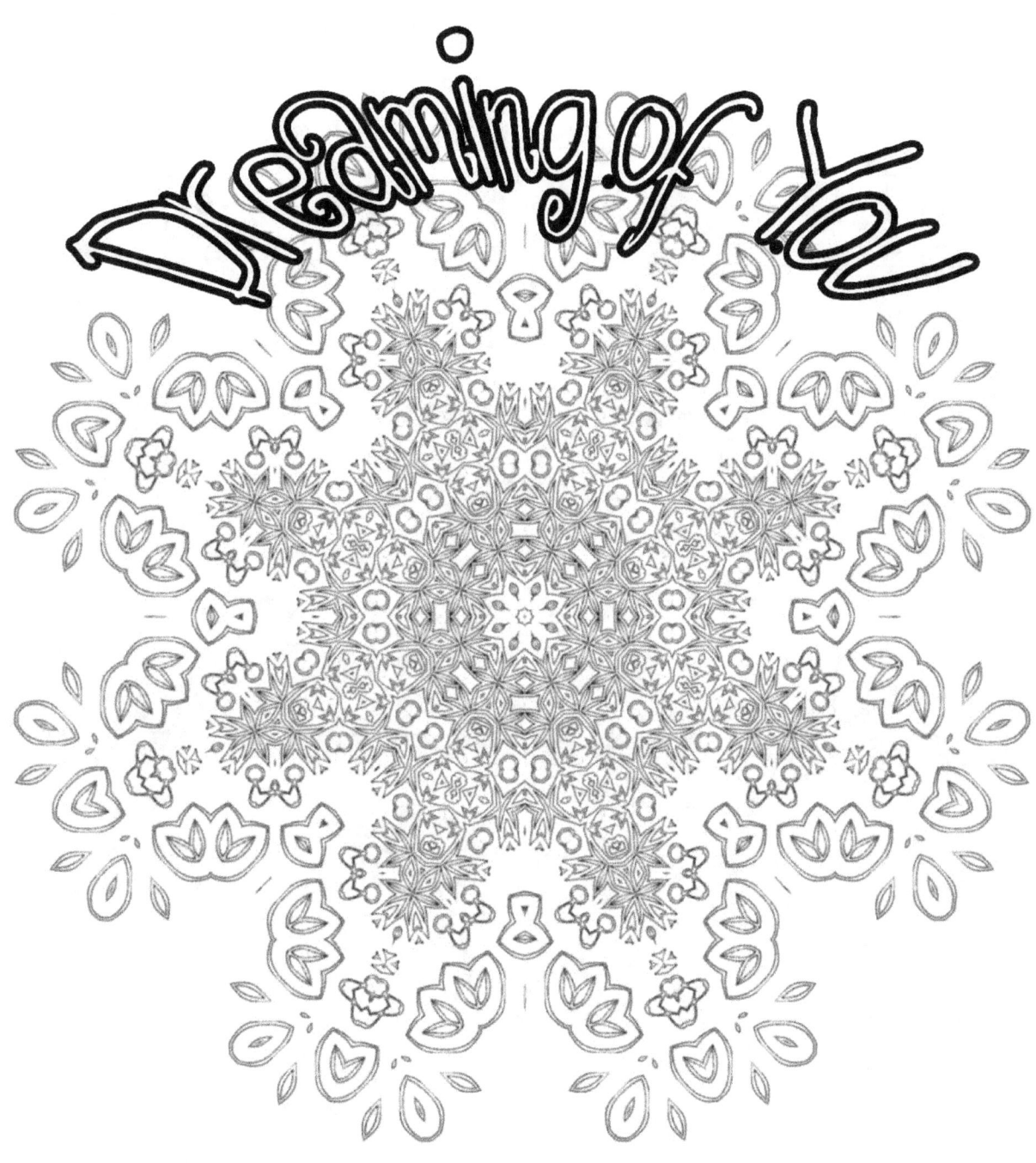

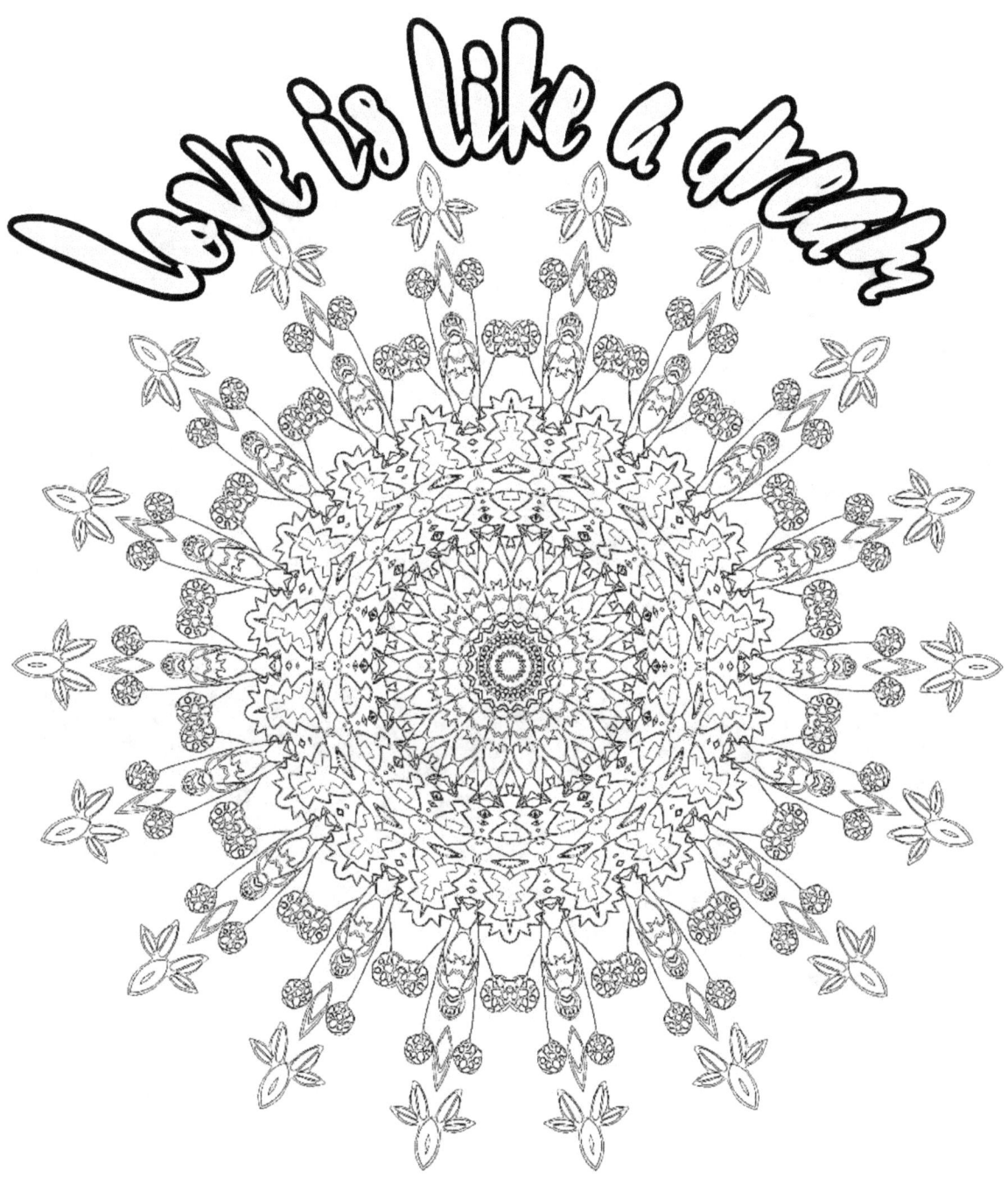

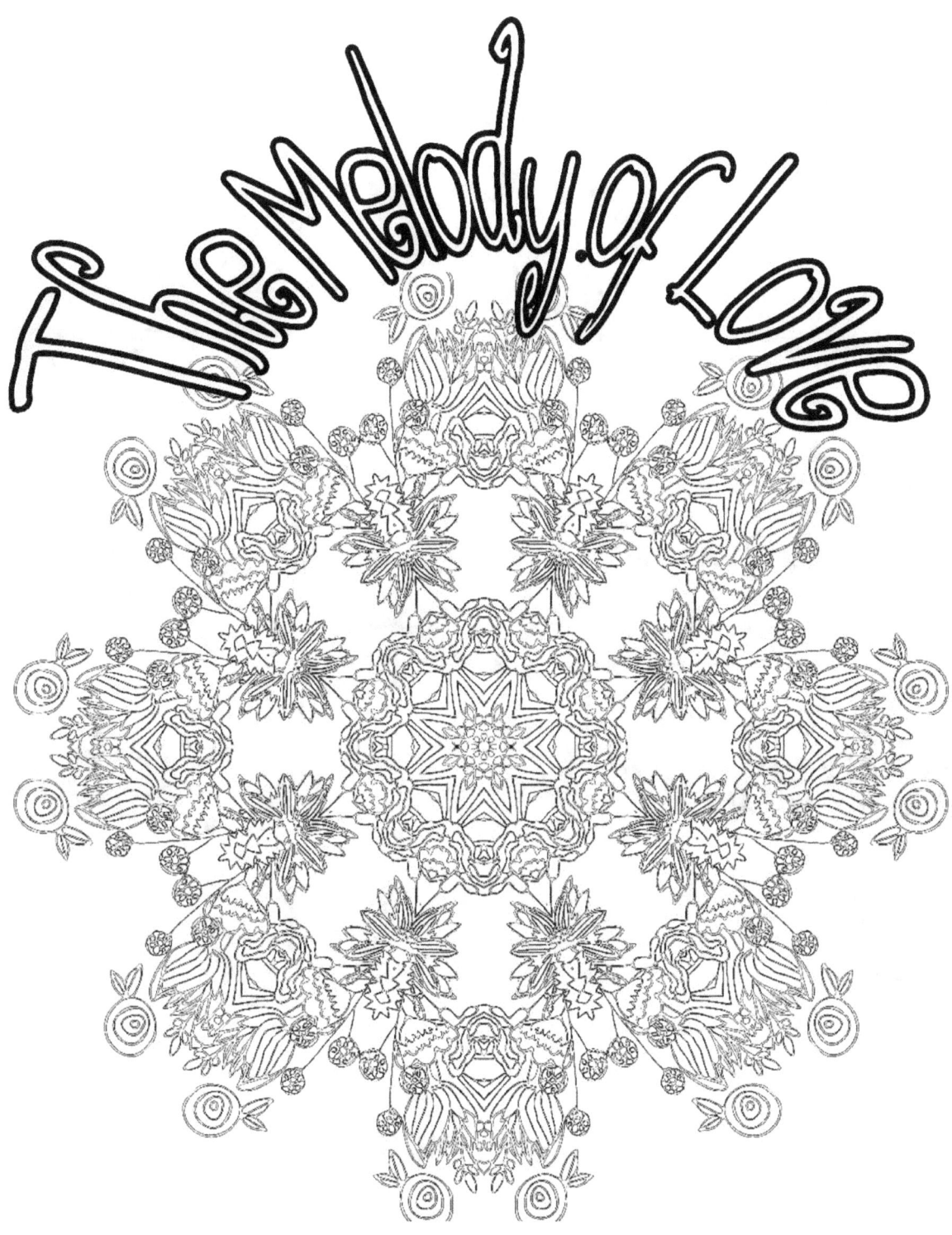

The Melody of Love

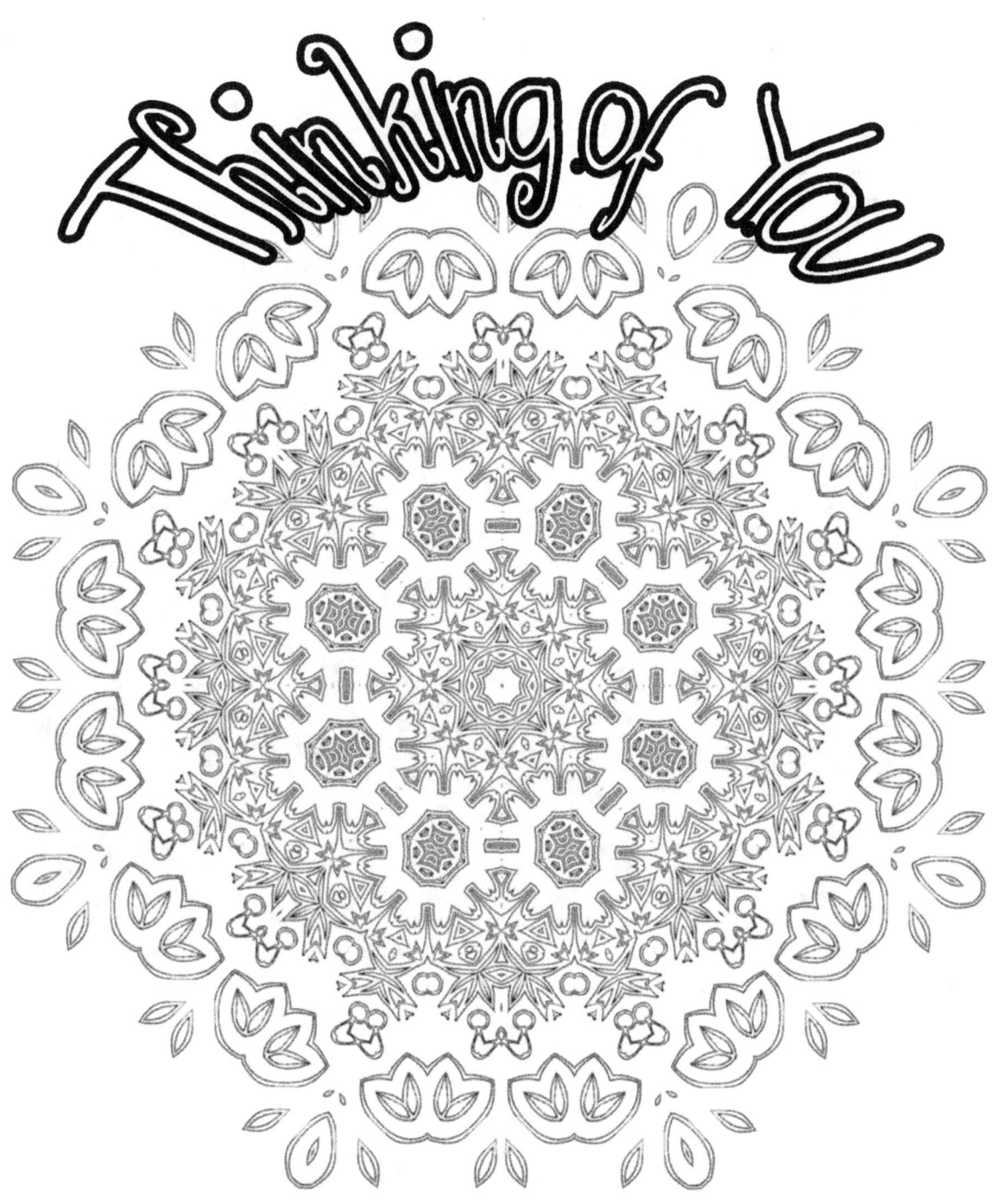

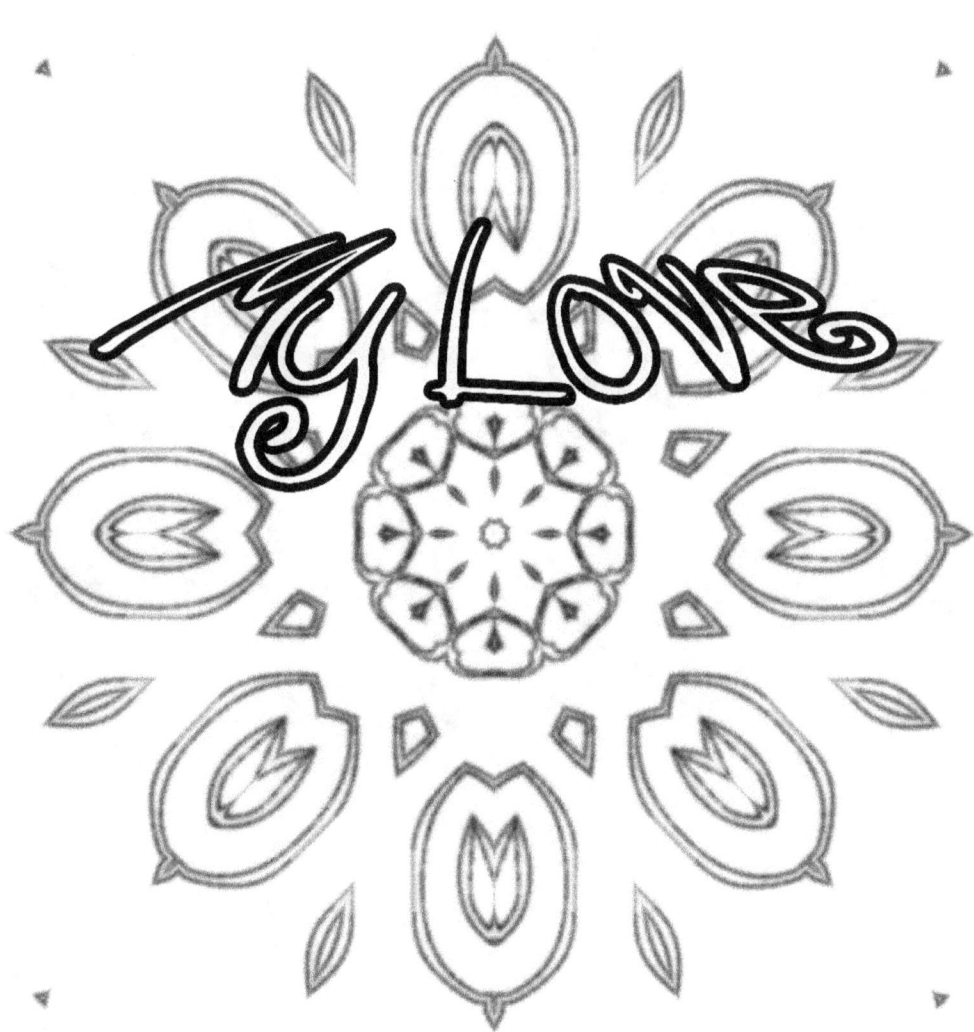

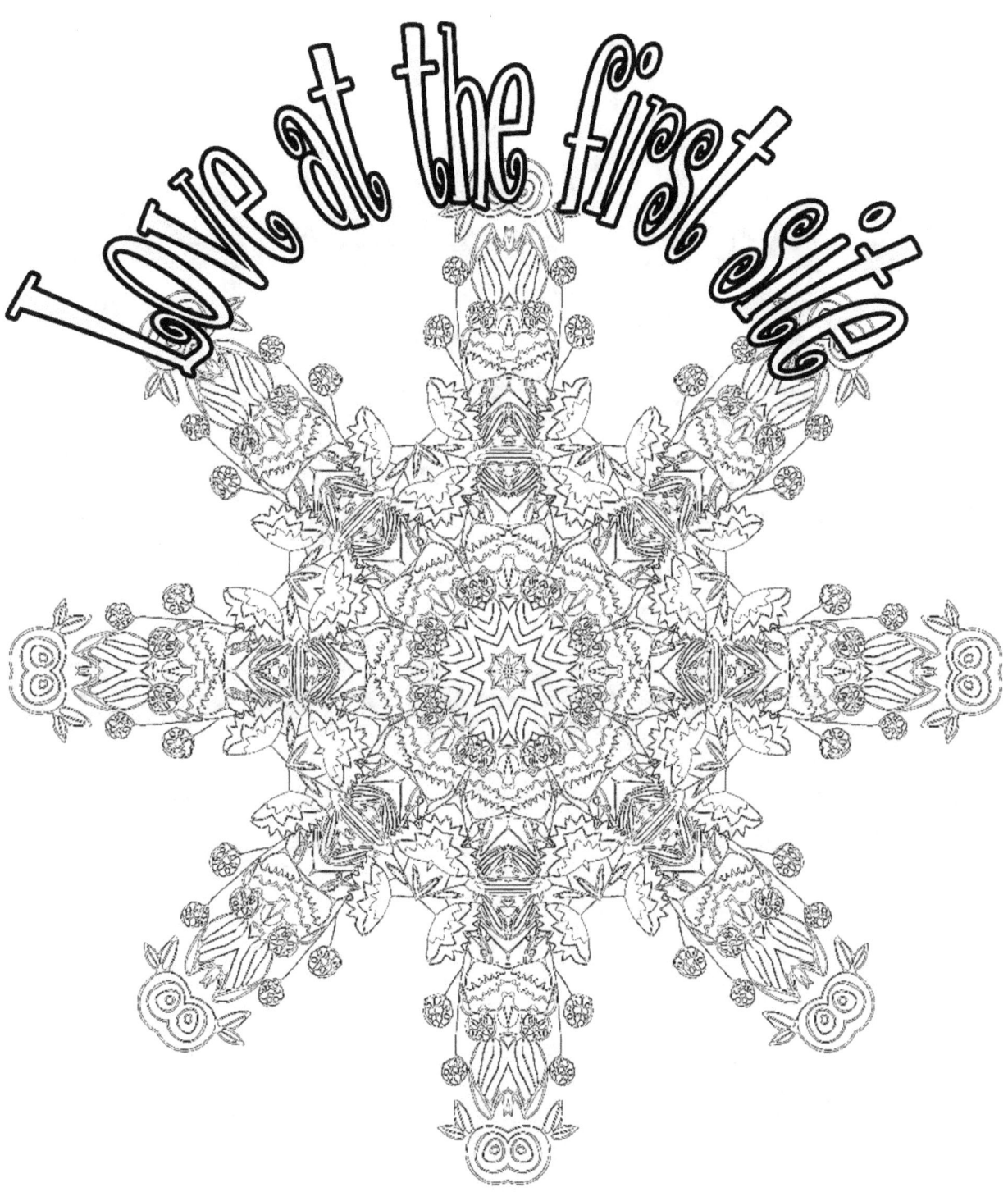

Love at the first site

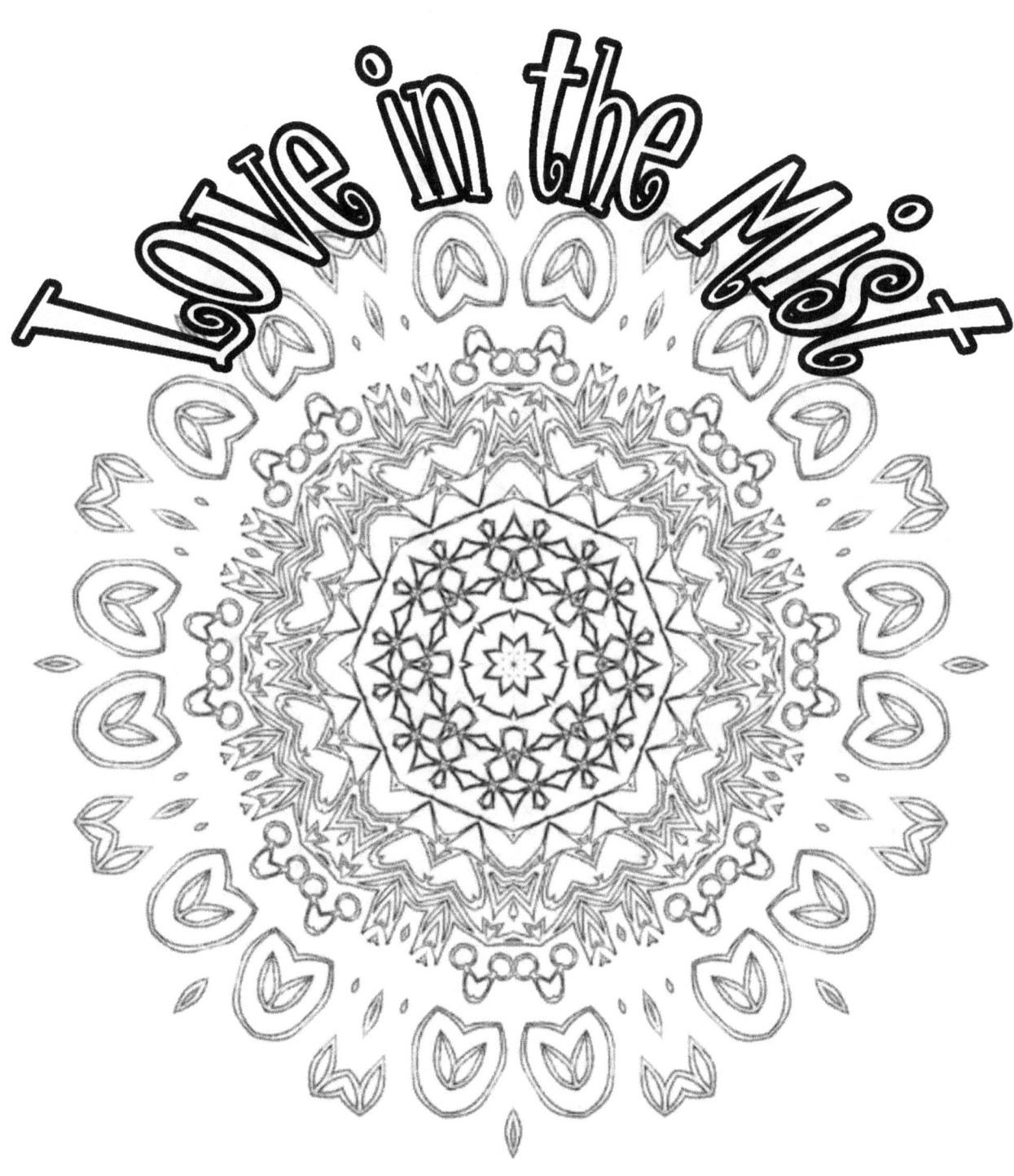

Love in the Mist

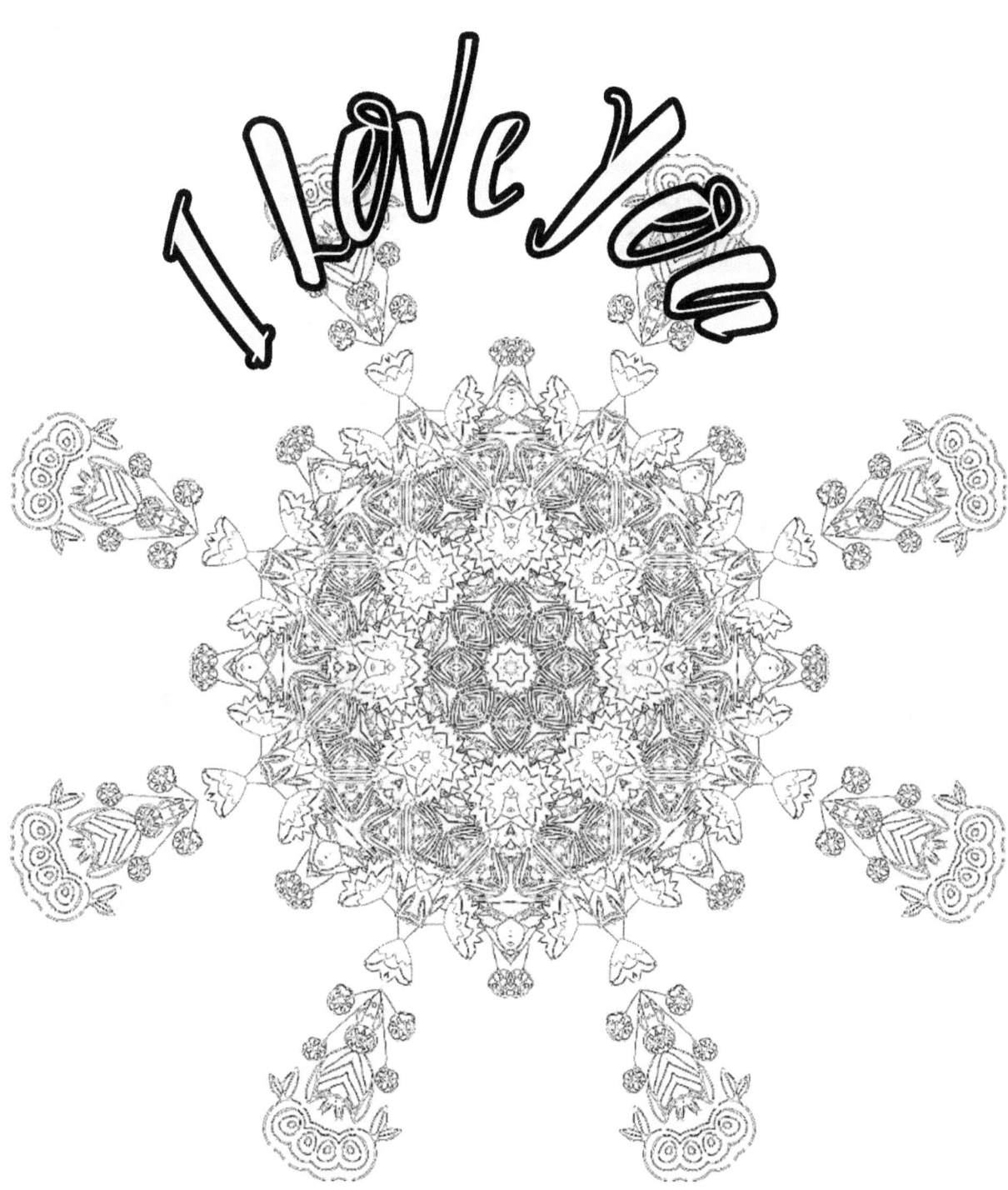

www.ingramcontent.com/pod-product-compliance
Lightning Source LLC
Chambersburg PA
CBHW081747170526
45167CB00009B/3959